MW01153921

OCEAN

BY BRENNA MALONEY

Children's Press®
An imprint of Scholastic Inc.

A special thank-you to the team at the Cincinnati Zoo & Botanical Garden for their expert consultation.

Copyright © 2024 by Scholastic Inc.

All rights reserved. Published by Children's Press, an imprint of Scholastic Inc., *Publishers since 1920*. SCHOLASTIC, CHILDREN'S PRESS, and associated logos are trademarks and/or registered trademarks of Scholastic Inc.

The publisher does not have any control over and does not assume any responsibility for author or third-party websites or their content.

No part of this publication may be reproduced, stored in a retrieval system, or transmitted in any form or by any means, electronic, mechanical, photocopying, recording, or otherwise, without written permission of the publisher. For information regarding permission, write to Scholastic Inc., Attention: Permissions Department, 557 Broadway, New York, NY 10012.

Library of Congress Cataloging-in-Publication Data available

ISBN 978-1-339-02075-4 (library binding) / ISBN 978-1-339-02076-1 (paperback)

10 9 8 7 6 5 4 3 2 1   24 25 26 27 28

Printed in China   62
First edition, 2024

Book design by Kay Petronio

Photos ©: cover top and throughout: Photography by Margriet Tilstra/Getty Images; 8 top: Gerard Soury/Getty Images; 8 center right: Kondor83/Getty Images; 9 center left: Reilly Wardrope/Getty Images; 9 center right: Peter Southwood/Wikimedia; 9 bottom: Tommi Kokkola Photography/Getty Images; 10-11 top: IBorisoff/Getty Images; 10-11 bottom: angel_nt/Getty Images; 16-17: Flip Nicklin/Minden Pictures; 18-19: Oregon Department of Fish & Wildlife/Flickr; 20-21: Adisha Pramod/Alamy Images; 22-23: 3dsam79/Getty Images; 24-25: atese/Getty Images; 26-27: Laura Hedien/Getty Images; 28-29: All Canada Photos/Alamy Images; 30 bottom center: Mike Hill/Getty Images; 30 bottom right: Gwenvidig/Getty Images.

All other photos © Shutterstock.

BLUE
SHARK

OCTOPUS

CONTENTS

WELCOME TO THE OCEAN

Earth is a watery world. Its nickname is the "blue planet." Did you know that water covers more than 70 percent of Earth's surface? Some places in the ocean are **shallow**, sunny, and warm. Others are deep, dark, and cold.

The ocean is a **habitat** with many different types of marine life. Scientists think there are about 700,000 **species** of animals living in the ocean!

FACT

"Ocean" and "sea" are not the same thing. A sea is a small area of an ocean, usually with land on several sides.

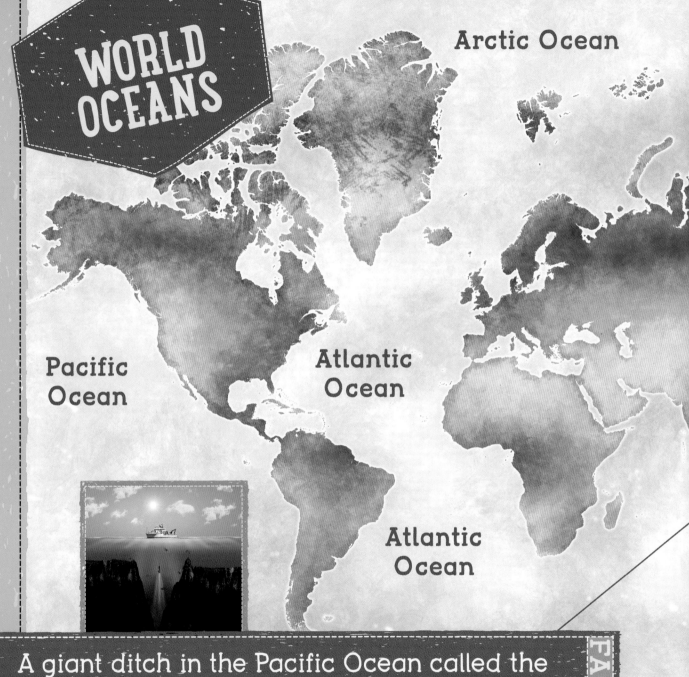

WORLD OCEANS

Arctic Ocean

Pacific
Ocean

Atlantic
Ocean

Atlantic
Ocean

A giant ditch in the Pacific Ocean called the
Mariana Trench is almost 7 miles (11 km) deep!

FACT

MARIANA
TRENCH

Pacific
Ocean

Indian
Ocean

Southern Ocean

WHERE IN THE WORLD?

Earth has five main oceans. From biggest to smallest, they are the Pacific, the Atlantic, the Indian, the Southern, and the Arctic Oceans. All these oceans are connected. Water flows between all of them as part of a single world ocean. Beneath the waves, there are mountains and bubbling volcanoes. Some of Earth's highest peaks and deepest ditches are found in the ocean.

LIFE IN THE OCEAN

BLUE SHARK

The ocean is swimming with life. About 85 percent of all plant life is found underwater. Kelp, seaweed, and algae are all found in the ocean. Some of Earth's smallest animals live there, too.

MORAY EEL

SEAWEED

OCTOPUS

BLUE WHALE

SEA TURTLE

SALPS

SEA LIONS

Creatures like **zooplankton** are so tiny they can be seen only with a microscope. Earth's largest animal—the blue whale—also lives in the ocean. Temperature, water depth, and distance from the shore all affect where plants and ocean animals live.

9

DAYTIME

NIGHTTIME

More people have traveled into space than have explored the deepest parts of the ocean.

FACT

DAY AND NIGHT

The ocean's surface receives the most sunlight. In the deep ocean, it can be hard to tell night from day. That's because the sun's light cannot reach below 0.6 miles (1,000 m) in the water. About 85 percent of the ocean is always dark and cold. Some ocean animals are **diurnal**. That means they are active by day. Other animals are **nocturnal**. They are active at night. Read on to find out what animals do as the day goes by!

BLUE SHARK

Blue sharks are early risers. They are always on the move. Their slim, rocket-shaped bodies glide through the water. At dawn, they look for **prey**. This is the best time to see them. The morning sun lights up prey swimming near the surface. From below, blue sharks can spot them easily and clearly. The sharks speed to the surface to eat squid, shrimp, lobster, and even seabirds.

FACT Blue sharks are named after their blue-tinted skin.

Sea lions can eat 40 pounds (18 kg) of food a day.

FACT

SEA LION

Above the waves, sea lions lie on rocks in the early morning sun. Then they dive into the water to swim and hunt. Sea lions are **carnivores**. They eat meat such as small fish and squid. They will eat almost any prey they can find. Sea lions will grab prey with their sharp teeth, then swallow it whole.

NARWHAL

Near the Arctic, narwhals often come to the surface during the day. Cracks in the sea ice above allow them to pop up for air when they need it. These "unicorns of the sea" have a long tusk on their heads. It's actually a tooth! It can grow as long as 10 feet (3 m). Narwhals may tap prey like squid or fish with their tusks to stun them before eating.

A narwhal is a type of whale.

Salps clean the ocean water as they eat.

FACT

SALP

It's evening in the ocean, just before the sun sets. A group of small ocean animals called salps make their way to the surface. The group forms a chain. Their bodies are mostly see-through. Salps hold the record for the world's largest animal **migration**. Why do they move? To eat, and to avoid being eaten. They rush to feed on tiny plants that live in the top few hundred feet of water.

IMMORTAL JELLYFISH

Immortal jellyfish are also active before the sun sets. But it's already dark farther down from the surface where they live. They are feeding on tiny floating plants and sea creatures. The immortal jellyfish looks like an ice cube with see-through strings. Even though "immortal" means to live forever, these jellyfish can not. But they can live for a very long time.

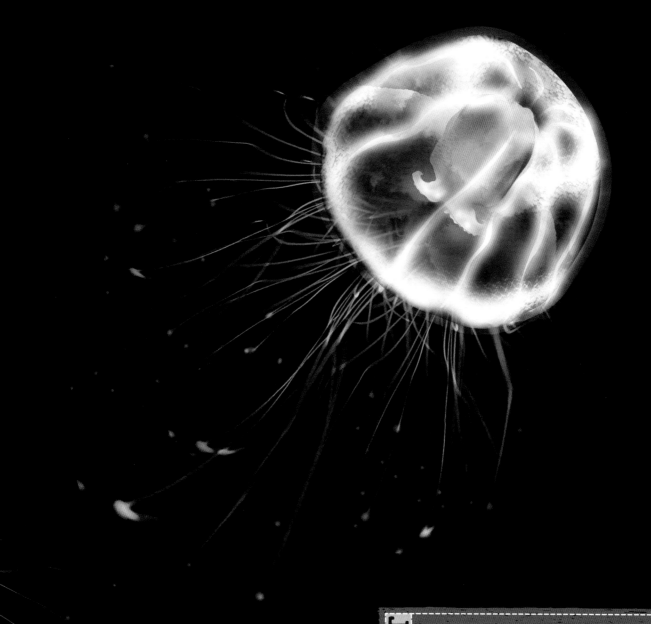

FACT Jellyfish don't have
a brain or a heart.

LANTERNFISH

Night is beginning to fall. The glow of a lanternfish lights up the ocean. These small fish become active at dusk. Parts of their heads, bellies, and tails give off light. It's called **bioluminescence**. The shine attracts other small fish the lanternfish can eat. Most lanternfish make a nightly journey up through the water, following zooplankton to eat.

NIGHTTIME

FACT Lanternfish have large eyes to help collect light in the dark water.

Octopuses have three hearts and blue-green blood.

FACT

OCTOPUS

It is nighttime on the ocean floor. An octopus can be seen "walking" along. It is nocturnal. This is its time to hunt. Using its eight arms, it scuttles along. It pauses at times to **camouflage** from prey. An octopus can match the color of its surroundings. It can also change the texture of its skin to hide itself. It spots a tasty clam, shrimp, lobster, or fish and eats it.

MORAY EEL

Moray eels hunt at night, too. Many live near the surface of the ocean. But these slippery fish are hard to spot, especially in the dark. They hide among the rough **coral** with only their heads showing. Moray eels breathe with their mouths open. They have long, sharp teeth. These nocturnal carnivores wait for a fish or crab to pass by. The moray eel shoots forward and snaps the prey up with its jaws.

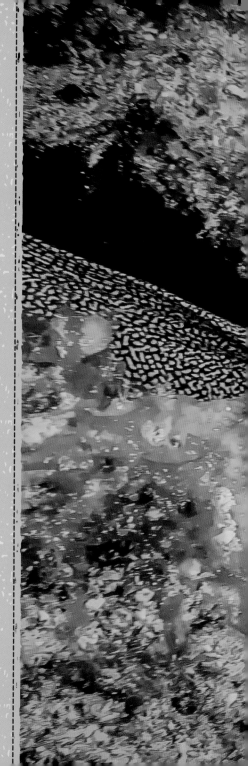

A baby eel is
called an elver.

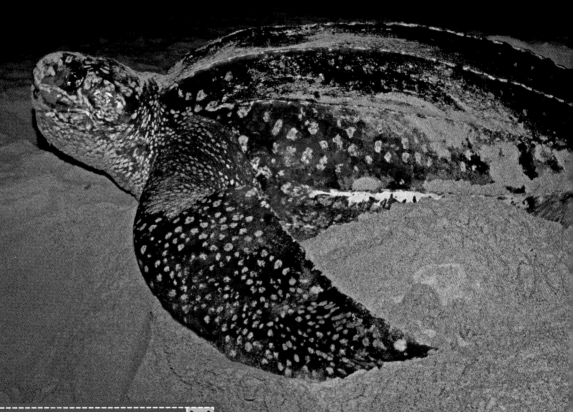

A group of turtle eggs is called a clutch.

SEA TURTLE

It is nighttime at the ocean's surface. A lone sea turtle slowly makes her way onto the sand by moonlight. She has an important job to do. She begins to dig a deep hole using her shovel-like back flippers. Here, she lays as many as 100 eggs. She covers the hole and walks back to the ocean. Within two months, her young will hatch at night. The hatchlings will head toward the water to start their lives in the ocean.

YOU DECIDE!

If you could choose, would you visit the ocean during the day or at night? To explore the surface, bring your wetsuit and dive in. You can see a lot of ocean life on the sunlit surface and just below the waves. If you would like to go deeper, grab your scuba gear. And to visit the ocean's depths, you may need a submarine. At home, you can learn even more about the ocean and the amazing animals who live there.

GLOSSARY

bioluminescence (bye-oh-loo-muh-NEH-suhns) the natural production of light by living creatures

camouflage (KAM-uh-flahzh) to disguise something so that it blends in with its surroundings

carnivore (KAHR-nuh-vor) an animal that eats meat

coral (KOR-uhl) a substance found underwater, made up of the skeletons of tiny sea creatures

diurnal (dye-UR-nuhl) active in the daytime

habitat (HAB-i-tat) the place where an animal or a plant is usually found

migration (mye-GRAY-shuhn) the movement of people or animals from one region or habitat to another

nocturnal (nahk-TUR-nuhl) active at night

prey (pray) an animal that is hunted by another animal for food

shallow (SHAL-oh) not deep

species (SPEE-sheez) one of the groups into which animals and plants are divided

zooplankton (zoh-uh-PLANGK-tuhn) a collection of small, passively floating, drifting, or somewhat mobile organisms occurring in a body of water

INDEX

Page numbers in **bold** indicate images.

ABOUT THE AUTHOR

Brenna Maloney is the author of dozens of books. She lives and works in Washington, DC, with her husband and two sons. She wishes she had more pages to tell you about oceans. She also wishes she had a cool tooth like a narwhal!